W9-AOC-512

DISCARD

MARGARET WISE BROWN

FOUR FUR FEET

Illustrated by Remy Charlip

Hyperion Books for Children
New York

Library of Congress Catalog Card No. 89-40210
ISBN 1-56282-213-6

About the author and artist . . .

MARGARET WISE BROWN published well over one hundred books in her short lifetime, including *Goodnight Moon, The Runaway Bunny,* and *David's Little Indian.* A number of stories that remained unpublished at her death have since been published, including *Four Fur Feet.* She was born in New York, and graduated from Hollins College in Virginia. For three years she was an editor of children's books at William R. Scott, Inc., Publisher.

REMY CHARLIP is an award-winning author/illustrator whose works for children have been praised for years. His colorful art is full of intricate shapes that attract and intrigue young minds. Mr. Charlip lives in New York City where he writes and illustrates children's books and works in children's theatre.

See the four fur feet
at the top of this page?
They are the feet part
of a furry animal.

Follow the animal's feet
around the pages of the book.
When you come to a picture
that looks wrong side up,
it's because the animal
has gotten part way
around the world.

Just turn the book around
and follow him
as he continues his walk
around the pages of the book
and around the world.

Oh, he walked around the world

on his four fur feet...

Oh, he walked around the world on his four fur feet,
his four fur feet, his four fur feet.
And he walked around the world on his four fur feet
and never made a sound—O.

Oh, he walked along the river on his four fur feet,
his four fur feet, his four fur feet.
He walked along the river on his four fur feet
and heard the boats go toot—O.

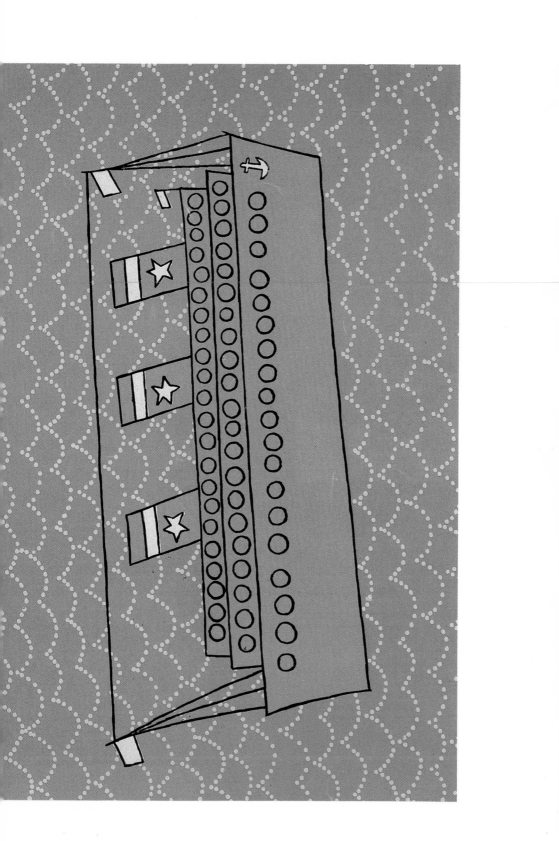

He walked by the railroad
on his four fur feet
and heard the trains go whoo—O.

Then he walked by the railroad
on his four fur feet,
his four fur feet, his four fur feet.

He walked into the country
on his four fur feet
and heard the cows go moo—O.

Then he walked into the country
on his four fur feet,
his four fur feet,   his four fur feet.

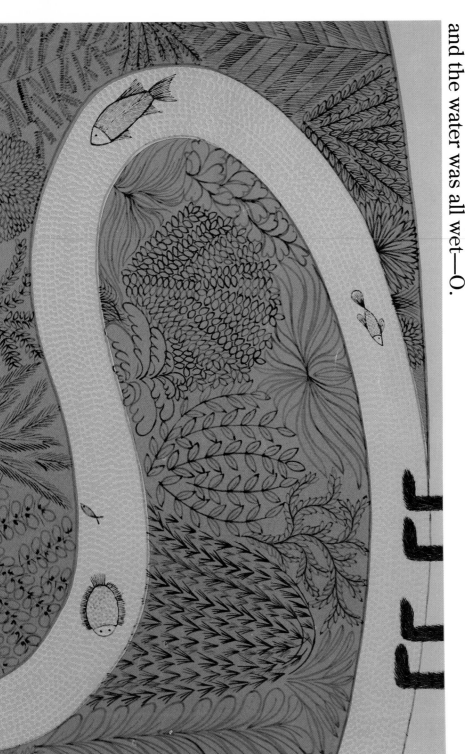

Then he waded down a stream on his four fur feet,
his four fur feet, his four fur feet.
He waded down a stream on his four fur feet,
and the water was all wet—O.

So he folded up his four fur feet,
his four fur feet, his four fur feet.

So he folded up his four fur feet
and lay down in the grass—O.

And the sun shone down on his four fur feet,
his four fur feet, his four fur feet.

And the sun shone down on his four fur feet
and made them feel all warm—O.

And as he slept he dreamed a dream,
dreamed a dream, dreamed a dream.

And as he slept he dreamed a dream
that all the world was round—O.

Oh, he walked around the world
on his four fur feet,
his four fur feet, his four fur feet.

And he walked around the world
on his four fur feet
and never made a sound—O.